$\mathscr{I}$n this book, **Warren Buffett: A Life of Inspiration**, you can peek into the exemplary life of Warren Buffett.

As known to many people worldwide, Warren Buffett is an epitome of success. His name appears consistently in the list of the wealthiest people around the globe. As of 2016, his net worth has gone up to an astounding amount. His net worth is now more than $66 billion.

In this book, you can take a closer look at his childhood days, the days when he faced a series of rejections, the days when he met the most important people in his life, his influential power as the leader of Berkshire Hathaway, and his timeless principles as an investor.

Here, you'll learn that Warren Buffett's success began when he was still young. He simply dreamed to make it big someday, and he did his part to wake up to a promising reality. He was determined, and as he matured, his determination didn't fall short.

While his immense wealth might be enough for others, he insists that life isn't all about money. He insists on being a well-rounded individual. Apart from being a focused entrepreneur, he also engages in other social causes.

He appreciates humanity, and strives to be a world-changer. Regardless of his hectic schedule, he hasn't forgotten the less fortunate ones. As his reputation goes, he's a leader in the world of philanthropy. He has wowed to give away 99% of his wealth over his lifetime.

Through the years, Warren Buffett valued his success. Regardless of the industry he chooses to delve in, he manages to be at the top. His fortune? It keeps on going up.

Without his unparalleled discipline, he might have taken a backseat – as an investor and as a responsible person. But, he's one-of-a-kind. He has always shown that he's more than willing to show excellence.

As you will learn from this book, Warren Buffett had his share of setbacks. Life doesn't exempt him from heartbreaks and disappointments. But, in spite of unfavorable circumstances, he rose above, and he managed to land at his current position: he's the chairman, CEO and the largest shareholder of Berkshire Hathaway.

Berkshire Hathaway is a multinational holding company for all of Buffett's investments. Today, Berkshire owns a diverse range of businesses that include insurance, retail, banking, rail road, newspaper publishing, jewelry sales, home furnishings as well as several regional electric and gas utilities. According to the 2016 Forbes Global 2000 list, Berkshire Hathaway is ranked as the fourth largest public company in the world.

Currently, Buffett is widely known as an elite investor. It's not known to many that he's more than that. In other aspects, such as healthcare, tax, renewable energy, and politics, he's not a stranger. His policies on certain issues are made public, and his straightforward mind is continually receiving admiration.

With a pile of accomplishments in various industries, it's as if success comes naturally to Warren Buffett. As you read his biography, you'll learn that it's not. Nevertheless, one thing's for sure:

Warren Buffett approaches life with the right attitude.

TABLE OF CONTENTS

Introduction

Chapter 1- The Man With A Vision...1

Life as a Child: Born as The One & Only.............................1

Determined to Make Money...3

Small & Short-Period Success, but Success Nonetheless...4

Investing & Practical Living: It's in the Genes...................5

Cruising through Elementary & High School.....................6

A Striking Interest in Stocks..7

The Beginning of Higher Pursuits....................................7

Aiming for Much Higher Pursuits.....................................9

Chapter 2 - Facing Adversities & Defying the Odds...........13

Meeting Rejection at the 1st Attempt.............................13

Shaking the Hands of Rejection Again............................14

Starting Anew & Almost Succeeding..............................16

A Quick Break..17

Ready to Rise...18

Having an Optimistic Character......................................20

Chapter 3- Friends & Partners for Life.............................23

A Lasting Bond with Bill Gates.......................................23

Donald Danly as among the 1st Business Partners......25

The Bond with "Cousin" Jimmy......................................26

A Lifelong Friendship with Katharine Meyer Graham..27

The Influence of Lorimer Davidson................................28

A Man Named William Ruane...29

Meeting Charlie..29

Chapter 4- Standing Tall: The Story of Becoming a Billionaire
....31

Making Millions..32

A New Leader..33

Life as a Billionaire...35

Retaining the Billion-Dollar Status....................36

Chapter 5- Sticking by Personal Principles as an Investor
.... 39

Familiarization with Personal Style...................39

On Transparency..40

Long-Term Plans..41

Always Thinking Clearly......................................42

Thinking as a Part-Owner...................................44

Understanding Personal Level of Competence..........45

Decisions Are Important......................................46

Trusting Gut Instincts..47

An Exit Strategy on Standby...............................48

Chapter 6- Keeping the Success Alive..................51

Appreciation for Life's Bounties.........................51

On Giving Back..52

On Looking Fear in the Eye................................53

Continually Investing in Himself.......................54

Always Valuing Money...54

Moving in the Right Direction............................56

Staying True to a Personal Definition of Success..........57

Conclusion...59

Thank You!

Education is our passport to the future, for tomorrow belongs to the people who prepare for it today."

-Malcolm X

$\mathcal{I}$ would like to thank you for downloading Warren Buffett: A Life of Inspiration. At **AmazingLivesForever**, our goal is to make history more accessible and enjoyable. I believe that reading biographies of successful personalities could provide some of the most valuable lessons in life.

ᴥ You might also Like... ᴥ

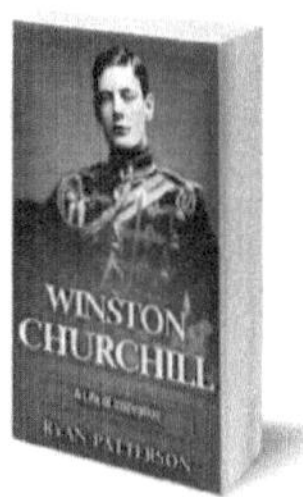

#1 Amazon Bestseller – Please click on the image above or visit the link below to get your copy.

https://www.amazon.com/dp/B01MRKG7ZA

I hope you enjoy these books and they inspire you on your journey to a better you.

Ryan

Chapter 1- The Man With A Vision

"Opportunities come infrequently. When it rains gold, put out the bucket, not the thimble."

-Warren Buffett

$\mathcal{W}$arren Buffett came into the world as a delight to his parents. He was born privileged, but not once had he entertained the idea of using his privilege as a one-way ticket to success. He learned to work, and he learned to work hard.

Even at such a juvenile age, he was outstanding. Not many boys his age were the least bit interested in establishing a bright foundation for themselves. Many boys preferred to play and remain happy-go-lucky. But, he wasn't like many boys.

Warren Buffett was one-of-a-kind.

⚜Life as a Child: Born as The One & Only⚜

The date was August 30, 1930. In a quiet town in Omaha, Nebraska, it was the day that Warren Buffett became the 2nd child of Howard Buffett and Leila Stahl Buffett.

Since his father, Howard, was a US Congressman, he set foot into the world as a disciplined young boy. He was taught the right values, and he learned to respect his parents.

Based on his old man's ways, he learned the importance of playing by the rules and avoiding petty trouble. He wasn't a rebel, and he understood the advantages of diplomacy.

With his parents' constant guidance, he stayed in school. He performed well academically. As a boy, he never given his folks a reason not to be proud.

But, although he was a dedicated schoolboy, he knew the meaning of fun too. With his father having Scandinavian roots, and his mother, having Spanish roots, he grew up with strong, reserved, ambitious, competitive, and steadfast influences.

Years later, Warren Buffett's mother gave birth to another child – a daughter. Warren Buffett is his parents' only son.

Together with his older sister, Doris, and his younger sister, *"Bertie"* or Roberta, he pursued adventurous bouts – adventurous business bouts, to be exact. It was as if his mind was filled with money-making ideas. It was as if he was chasing a "high" whenever he ran after profitable opportunities.

His parents hadn't pushed him to work, but he refused to hide his business-minded side. Even as a youngster, he exhibited a deep fascination for math, investments, and entrepreneurial ventures. Who would've expected that decades later, he would earn the reputation *"The Oracle or The wizard of Omaha"*?

⚘Determined to Make Money⚘

Warren Buffett was never groomed by his parents to engage in different business ventures as a child. Instead, his parents granted him the freedom to be a normal boy. His determination to make money shone through upon seeing his parents experience hard times to make ends meet.

He was born with a silver spoon, but his privileged life faded not long after it began. A few months before he could celebrate his 1st birthday, the bank that kept his family's savings closed. The elder members of the family hadn't prepared themselves for such a situation and hence had to cut down and limit their luxuries.

For one, his mother had to alter her ways for a while. His mother had to be more conservative. For him, it was heartbreaking to see her like that. He witnessed her skipping dinner for his father to have a full meal. And, although she was a religious person and a woman of routine, she had to sacrifice attending church and accomplishing other activities.

From that point on, Warren Buffett's ambition to get rich became apparent. He didn't want to see his family members stick to a tight lifestyle because there was no other choice. From then on, he expressed a formidable statement.

He decided that he was going to be a millionaire before he turned 30. Otherwise, he'd jump off the tallest building in Omaha!

For him, it was about granting a good life to his family. And, for him, it wasn't all about making money. Rather, it was about the fun of it – of making money and watching the amount grow.

⚘Small & Short-Period Success, but Success Nonetheless⚘

"Rule No. 1: Never lose money. Rule No. 2: Never forget rule No.1."

Warren Buffett was recorded speaking such words at a later point in life. But, even when he was still at a juvenile stage, it was no secret: he valued money.

After all, he was born during the Great Depression. The Great Depression hit Omaha, Nebraska – and it hit it hard. Like most kids that grew up during the period, he learned to value money.

These were his initial gigs to earn income:

- He delivered weekly newspapers door-to-door.

- He sold Coca Cola bottles, chewing gum, and stamps.

- He delivered Washington Post papers and earned $175 monthly.

- He worked in his grandpa's grocery store.

- (Together with a friend), he invested $100 in a pinball machine and installed it in a small barber's shop. Since the business venture proved a success, he invested in several more of these pinball machines and installed them in 2 more barber's shops. Later, a war veteran bought the business.

Due to his menial gigs, he was able to accumulate $1,200 as savings. He was a boy at that time alright, but he exhibited unparalleled wisdom when it came to spending money.

With the $1,200 in his savings account, Warren Buffett boldly purchased land of his own. When a 40-acre farm became available, he knew that it was too good of a deal to miss.

✎ Investing & Practical Living: It's in the Genes✎

If dared to perform a lengthy mathematical calculation in his head (without a pen and paper or calculator), Warren Buffett is capable of impressing crowds.

By the looks of it, he inherited his mathematical proficiency from his mother. She was exceptional at math, and his performance in school revealed that he wasn't short of math skills, too.

In addition, his father made a significant contribution to his character, too. By serving as an example, he was the receiving end of his father's lessons on practical living.

Warren Buffett's father was a practical man. His wisdom (when it came to accumulating the right utilities) was undeniable.

For one, after World War II, his father invested money in tangible assets. His father knew that inflation was accelerating at that time, and he knew that prices were about to drop. Among the assets he bought were a crystal chandelier, silver sterling flatware, and gold coins. He also purchased a farm and kept a supply of canned goods!

Warren Buffett once told aspiring entrepreneurs:

"If you buy things you don't need, you're soon going to sell the things you need."

His father's influence was the primary reason he became a wise investor. Particularly, his father's influence was the reason why he still prefers tangible assets over intangible ones.

Overall, he turned out to be so successful due to the guidance of his parents.

↶ Cruising through Elementary & High School ↷

Warren Buffett's initial schooling was at the Rose Hill Elementary School. There, he settled down for a while. He learned the basics. He even be-friended a few kids, whom he soon bade farewell to.

He had to say goodbye to his small life in Omaha. It was a family decision.

Come 1942, his father won the national elections, and was elected to the first of his 4 terms in the US Congress. Since his father's victory also meant his family's victory, the Buffett family moved to Washington, DC.

There, he proceeded with his elementary and high school education. He attended 2 new schools, Alice Deal Junior High School and Woodrow Wilson High School.

When he finished high school, his classmates weren't oblivious to his eventual route. Below his yearbook picture was a caption. It read: *"[He] likes Math. [He's] a future stockbroker."*

✺A Striking Interest in Stocks✺

Near the brokerage of Warren Buffett's father was a regional stock brokerage. Inside was a cozy lounge for customers.

Guess whose hangout was it.

Warren Buffett's! His interest in stocks and the overall operations of the stock market was quite apparent.

"By the age of 10, I'd read every book in the Omaha public library about investing, some twice. You need to fill your mind with various competing thoughts and decide which make sense. Then you have to jump in the water – take a small amount of money and do it yourself. Investing on paper is like reading a romance novel vs. doing something else. You'll soon find out whether you like it. The earlier you start, the better," he shared.

When he had a chance to see the wonders of New York City for the 1st time, he made it a mission to visit the New York Stock Exchange. He even bought stocks!

When he had enough money at age 11, Warren Buffett bought a total of 6 shares from Citgo Petroleum Corporation (formerly Cities Service). With his older sister sharing his enthusiasm for investments, he split all 6 shares with her. 3 were for himself, and the other 3 were for his sister.

✺The Beginning of Higher Pursuits✺

At the age of 14, Warren Buffett filed his 1st tax return. He tasted success as a young businessman and he was doing well academically. Then, he also reached his short-term financial goals.

With his achievements then, it was apparent that he was a responsible boy. He dreamed big, and he thought of going at additional successes one step at a time.

When he finished high school, Warren Buffett decided that it was time to move up the ladder with his ventures. He decided that it was time to aim higher.

Come 1947, he applied to the University of Pennsylvania's prestigious venue for the elite business-minded bunch: The Wharton School. He got accepted, of course.

While it was a privilege, attending the University of Pennsylvania's The Wharton School wasn't his idea. In fact, had he been granted his ways, he wouldn't have passed up the opportunity to focus solely on his business ventures. For him, he already had what it would take to look success in the eye.

It was his father who wanted him to pursue a degree in the reputable business school. And, because he respected his old man, he stepped up. He followed the advice.

He left Omaha and eyed a place in Pennsylvania. He settled in and in a matter of time, he enrolled at UPenn.

He appreciated being in The Wharton School. He appreciated the honor it brought him. When he got the chance to maximize his college experience, he happily obliged. There, he swore to a brotherhood.

Alpha Sigma Phi was the fraternity Warren Buffett joined. With great regard to honor and tradition, his fraternity brothers made his stay colorful.

Unfortunately, though, the enthusiasm wasn't enough to make his time at the university last. He liked it there, but he decided to head back home.

After two years at The Wharton School, he transferred. From the state of Pennsylvania, he moved back to his hometown. There, he submitted an application to another prestigious school: The University of Nebraska-Lincoln. He was admitted.

At the fine age of 19, he was a proud graduate. The elite school credited him with a Bachelor of Science degree in Business

Administration.

⌁ Aiming for Much Higher Pursuits ⌁

Warren Buffett recognized success, and he knew that he was tasting it. Since he'd always be triumphant with his business ventures, he already had an idea of how to play his cards.

With his degree in Business Administration, he began to see himself chasing after bigger affairs. He enrolled at the Columbia Business School, and worked for a Master of Science degree in Economics. Once he graduated, he eyed another school: The New York Institute of Finance.

The New York Institute of Finance is a company that provides high-level education - with the New York Stock Exchange as its founder. There, he met like-minded individuals. The esteemed school didn't disappoint him. Its trademark motto, *"Where Wall Street goes to school"*, is a definition of the place. It was where the top professionals in the industry of finance gained their wisdom.

At The New York Institute of Finance, he learned to take his finesse with money to a whole new level. What exactly had he learned there? To be a strategic entrepreneur, to devise flawless investing concepts, and to be relentless in pursuing opportunities, to name a few.

There, he was taught to stand on his own two feet. There, he realized that the chance to be better was all his. He realized the benefits of going further.

There, it dawned on him that he had to branch out and to start maximizing his earning potential. Thus, he mustered the courage to do so.

He made a pact: not to stop working. He learned to always maximize his time and profitability. In other words, he told himself that he needed to be active, and to keep his income actively flowing. When he was 20 years old, he earned (and saved) almost $10,000.

He worked at different companies, too. He may be the type who works for the long haul, but he also understood that he had to make adjustments regularly. For 3 years, he signed up as an investment salesman at Buffett-Falk and Co. He then resigned to take a job as a securities analyst at Graham-Newton Corporation for 2 years.

Although he valued his employment with the aforementioned companies, he decided to part from them and to pursue higher positions. With his positions from his previous employers, he hadn't experienced major problems.

But, he realized that he could still do better. Due to his diligence, he eventually found better.

Come 1956, he welcomed the opportunity as a general partner at Buffett Partnership, Ltd. With him as the co-operator, the company flourished. Apart from inspiring his fellows to always be practical, he was stern when it came to his money-making ways.

With his career's boom, he was satisfied. He pictured himself being even more successful for years to come.

When he turned 25, his net worth was valued at $200,000. By then, it occurred to him that he had loads of money. In fact, he had all the money he needed. If someone else were in his shoes with his riches, that person would've chosen the easy way out. That person would've settled for the good life with his current wealth.

Warren Buffett could've chosen the easy way out. For an average man, his current money was more than enough to live a fairly pleasant life. He could've gone for a vacation, or spent his money on a house, car, and other luxuries.

But, of course, he didn't do all that. He was never easily tempted to ignore his principles. He had always lived in adherence to his frugal ways. He wasn't one to spend all of his savings – unless he could establish (at least) another income source.

Importantly, he was a man with big dreams, and he was one

who always believed in himself. Once, he was quoted with these words:

"I always knew I was going to be rich. I don't think I ever doubted it for a minute."

Even before he set out for bigger pursuits, it was already clear to him. To him, it was no secret that he was already quite rich, but he hadn't wanted to be just rich.

Instead, he longed to be filthy rich – or wealthy, to put it in more apt terms. He believes that with a stream of money, he's granted plenty of options. He can use it for himself, and even share it with others.

Come 1962, due to his persevering character, Warren Buffett became a billionaire. Today, he remains one of the richest people worldwide.

"Someone's sitting in the shade today because someone planted a tree a long time ago"

– Warren Buffett

When it comes to his ambitions, Warren Buffett is fervent. He dreams big, and despite rejections, he continues to dream big.

When matters turn out unexpectedly, he chooses to stay still, and he chooses to try again. Having a stroke of bad fortune doesn't easily discourage him. He understands that disappointments are unavoidable.

Fortunately, a fervent spirit is favorable to success – especially as a stock broker. And, a fervent spirit is part of the formula that got him quite far in life.

✒Meeting Rejection at the 1st Attempt✒

Back when The University of Nebraska-Lincoln granted him a Bachelor of Science degree, Warren Buffett felt proud of himself. Like most graduates, he recognized the thrill in accomplishing a major feat. Since he longed to remain proud of himself, he embarked on another goal for his education.

If you think his 1st choice was Columbia for his Master's, it may come off as a surprise that it wasn't. He was ambitious, and he targeted another school in the Ivy League: Harvard University.

Unfortunately, after submitting an application to Harvard's admission office, he knew he had to consider alternatives upon the receipt of a rejection letter. In retrospect, he might've been crushed by the rejection, but he wasted no time for self-pity. He was set to get back on his feet.

Warren Buffett's resiliency showed itself when he chose not to let his rejection from Harvard impede his quest. Instead of staying down, he eyed other options. He was about to attend another prestigious school, and he had to make it happen.

As he evaluated his options, he recognized a name that he had a high regard for. He recognized a name that embodied a professional investor. The man was Benjamin Graham and he was a professor at the Columbia Business School.

Since he deemed Benjamin Graham highly, the decision was made. In a way, the rejection from Harvard University granted him the opportunity to see what else was out there.

And, that's exactly what he did. He saw what else was waiting for him. A few months later, he was off to Columbia Business School!

⚭Shaking the Hands of Rejection Again⚭

Warren Buffett appreciated the teachings of Benjamin Graham. He realized that his path to success could be made even brighter with an educator like Graham in his midst. Years after his time at Columbia Business School, he approached his teacher once more.

As he usually prefers, he insists on having good people as peers. He appreciates people with positive influences. Once, he was quoted saying:

"It's better to hang out with people better than you. Pick out associates whose behavior is better than yours and you'll drift in that direction."

Back then, he wanted to be around Benjamin Graham's company. As he discovered that Graham was a board member of an American Insurance Company, Government Employees Insurance Company or GEICO, it was a light bulb moment for him.

Since he considered it a great opportunity to work with Benjamin Graham, Warren Buffett took a train. His destination was the headquarters of the Government Employees Insurance Company in Washington, DC.

It was a Saturday and he found that the office was closed. He knocked on the door till a janitor allowed him to enter. After enquiring if anyone was still working, he was led to a man on the sixth floor. This man, Lorimer Davidson, was the Head of Investments at that time and would later go on to become the CEO of GEICO.

Buffett and Davidson spent many hours that day engaged in profound discussions about the insurance business. None of them realized at that time the huge impact this meeting would later have on the company. For Buffett, the conversation with Davidson increased his self-confidence. More importantly, it somehow validated his ability of possibly working in the insurance business; he learnt enough to make his first purchase of GEICO stock.

After putting his talk with Davidson to rest, Warren Buffett approached Benjamin Graham. To the educator, he made a proposal – and an irresistible one. His enthusiasm when it came to working with Graham could hardly be concealed. Under the educator's authority, he offered to work for free.

But, being enthusiastic about a work opportunity wasn't enough. He was turned down.

Benjamin Graham hadn't undermined Warren Buffett, at all. The teacher realized his potential to be one of the greats.

For Graham, Buffett was still a "fresh" individual. For the educator, the student needed to be seasoned with experience – and only the student could get that experience.

✄Starting Anew & Almost Succeeding✄

Warren Buffett refused to dwell on his rejection from Benjamin Graham. It made him less confident, yes, but it hadn't been a major roadblock. He packed his bags, bid adieu to Washington, DC, and returned to Omaha.

Back in his hometown, his odds started turning around. He made a name for himself as a stockbroker. He devoted his energy and time to his work.

Alongside, he kept himself occupied with purposeful activities. He registered for a public speaking course that addressed the philosophies of a respected influential figure, Dale Carnegie.

This public speaking course shaped him to be even more confident in life. He challenged himself to teach a class at the University of Nebraska. In a matter of time, he became an educator of a night class called "Investment Principles".

Being an educator at the University of Nebraska required a lot of confidence. Why? On an average, the age of his students was twice his own age.

Because he could handle teaching, his confidence granted him encouragement. With about $10,000 in his account, he made a bold decision to use $2,000.

As a side investment, Buffett purchased a gas station. Particularly, he purchased a Sinclair Texaco gas station. But, the investment didn't work out and eventually he ended up losing 20% of his money.

✄A Quick Break✄

Since he encountered another failure in his attempt to go far, he decided to rest for a bit.

The failures hadn't left him unaffected. But, he never entertained the idea of entirely putting an end to his quest of achieving bigger goals. For a brief period, however, he decided to take it easy.

For Buffett, it has always been important to know the right time to take a backseat. His goal is to move forward always, but he doesn't fail to acknowledge the benefits of breaks.

Fast forward to his successful years today, Warren Buffett carries this mindset. In fact, he (together with a partner) popularized the word *"assiduity"*. The word means the ability to simply sit around and do nothing.

One of his remarkable quotes about doing nothing goes like this:

"You do things when the opportunities come along. I've had periods in my life when I've had a bundle of ideas come along, and I've had long dry spells. If I get an idea next week, I'll do something. If not, I won't do a damn thing."

For a short while, that's exactly what he did. He stopped introducing stressful situations to his life, and instead, he focused on other parts of his life.

It was in 1952 when he got married at a local church along Underwood Avenue, Dundee Presbyterian Church. The marriage was to a civil rights activist, cabaret singer, and entrepreneur, Susan Thompson.

A year after, he and his wife introduced the world to their 1st child. They had a daughter named Susan Alice.

Another year after, when Warren Buffett was settled down, he received excellent news. It was the news that he hadn't anticipated.

Benjamin Graham approached him. The educator offered him a job at Graham-Newman Corporation with a starting salary of $12,000 a year. As he had long considered working with Benjamin Graham an honor, he happily accepted.

✄Ready to Rise✄

With a family of his own and a job at Benjamin Graham's

partnership, Warren Buffett realized that things were lining up in his favor. But, as past events had taught him, he needed to let his feet stay on the ground.

Although chasing after bigger goals wasn't a fault, he learned to be appreciative of his current employment. Instead of aiming for another investment, he chose to be focused even more on his current undertakings.

Particularly, he focused on his job at Benjamin Graham's partnership. In a way, he didn't have a choice. To keep his job, he had to excel, and to excel, he had to focus.

Benjamin Graham was a superb educator at Columbia Business School. As it turned out, he was also a superb boss. He could be rather tough, but he was superb, nonetheless.

At Graham-Newman Corporation, Warren Buffett worked closely with prominent investors. Most of these prominent investors' names were synonymous to success.

One of these names belonged to Walter Schloss.

Walter Schloss was a wise colleague. He hadn't attended college, but his thinking outsmarted that of many. He was a reputable investor who had thought-provoking concepts of stocks.

As colleagues, Walter Schloss and Warren Buffett engaged in profound arguments. A notable argument bordered on stocks providing a wide margin of safety in terms of intrinsic value and price.

The aforementioned argument was notable since it left Buffett with questions. He wondered about the stock market's criteria with regard to Graham-Newman Corporation's operations. Were the criteria too rigid? And, due to this rigid criteria, was Graham's partnership missing out on other features?

His work relationship with Walter Schloss allowed him to sharpen his mind. He remained inquisitive, and it ensured that his interest in the stock market lingered on.

Being in a stable position in his job, he worried less about uncertainties in life. A couple of months after he settled in at Graham's partnership, he and his wife had another child.

This time, the 2nd child was a boy. Due to the wondrous influences of Benjamin Graham on him, Warren Buffett named his son Howard Graham.

He was proud to be one of Benjamin Graham's loyal disciples. After 2 years of working there, however, he had to go.

Benjamin Graham, who was 62 years old at that time, decided to retire. With the partner's approval, he ended the partnership.

For Warren Buffett, this was bad news. His time at the partnership was eventful. It also made him realize that he had more than $174,000 as personal savings. That meant a new opportunity: he could open a partnership of his own!

꒰Having an Optimistic Character꒱

After saying goodbye to Graham-Newman Corporation, Warren Buffett began Buffett Partnership Ltd. A bit later, he branched out and operated 2 more partnerships.

By then, he realized that it was time. He realized that it was time to flex his frugal ways. He rewarded himself by purchasing a brand new house!

For $31,500, a 5-bedroom stucco house caught his attention. It was big and cozy enough for a growing family. It was not too expensive also. Best of all, it was located in Omaha!

By the looks of it, matters were moving smoothly for him. Due to that, he and his wife felt that it was time to introduce an addition to their family.

Warren Buffett's 3rd child was born in 1958. He gave his new son the name Peter Andrew.

He spent sufficient time with his family. At the same time, he provided for them. This meant that while he was a family man, his dedication to his career stayed.

The thought of retirement occurred to him, then. After all, he was not exactly in financial turmoil. Plus, his family could live a comfortable life with his funds.

For a while, he pictured himself taking it easy from that point on. But, he remembered his childhood goal: he had to be a millionaire. To achieve the long-time goal, he realized that retirement wasn't an option.

Around the time of his 3rd child's birth, he operated another 3 partnerships. Overall, within just 3 years of leaving Graham-Newman Corporation and creating a mark for himself, he was able to handle 6 partnerships.

With the series of successes, Warren Buffett's general outlook was noticeable. In retrospect, he was not immune to rejections. He had his share of getting his confidence level pulled down.

The way he persists on bouncing back and standing tall is admirable. Instead of turning away, he gathers himself and continues walking – as if no obstacle is tossed along his way.

Chapter 3- Friends & Partners for Life

*"Tell me who your heroes are and I'll tell you who
you'll turn out to be."*

-Warren Buffett

As a practical man, Warren Buffett was quite selective regarding his engagements. This was also the case when it came to his peers.

If he were to spend time with people, he wanted to be in the company of those who were great influences on him. He preferred to share memorable moments with those who could contribute to the betterment of his well-being.

With luck on his side, he stumbled across notable peers. For decades, he could continue to count on them.

✂A Lasting Bond with Bill Gates✂

In July 1991, Warren Buffett had a special appointment. He was set to meet a 35-year-old celebrated businessman, philanthropist, and co-founder of Microsoft.

Little had he known that Bill Gates wasn't the least bit interested in meeting him. If Gates' mother hadn't forced him, there'd be no such meeting.

"I don't think we'd have much in common," Bill Gates told his mother, then.

Fate had its way as Bill Gates' mother intervened. She wanted the meeting to happen. And, of course, it did.

With a shared interest in business and philanthropy, the two men hit it off. Until now, both of them continue to learn from each other. Considering the value that they contribute to each other's personal and professional lives, they continue to maintain their friendship.

Due to enlightenment from each other, they understand some matters more clearly. They have like-minded perspectives on the world. Hours would pass by after they begin to engage in conversations.

When they discussed all sorts of ideas, neither one treated the other with privileges – as if they have no clue that they were both successful businessmen.

Warren Buffett and Bill Gates learned to appreciate one another. Both of them learned to invest in their friendship.

As Bill Gates once said, perhaps the biggest lesson he acquired from more than two decades of knowing Warren Buffett is about the power of friendship. Since the day they first met, they discovered that learning and laughing are activities that can't be overdone.

Bill Gates even shares these remarkable words about the investor:

- "Even though he keeps up a hectic schedule, Warren finds time to nurture friendships like few other people I know."

- "It's about being the kind of friend you wish to have."

- "He goes out of his way to make people feel good about themselves and share his joy about life."

- "Everyone should be lucky enough to have a friend who is as thoughtful and kind as Warren."

⚜Donald Danly as among the 1st Business Partners⚜

Wilson Coins Operated Machines was among Warren Buffett's 1st business ventures. In 1947, when he was still at school in Omaha, Buffett came up with an idea of buying up second hand pinball machines and placing them in nearby barber shops. He got his friend Donald Danly to help with refurbishing the pinball machines and Danly, thus, became his first business associate. The business prospered and together they learned that business was good as long as the operators had the right attitude.

Buffett and Danly were a great pair. For their business venture's success, they trained themselves to think big and always strategize. They designated the required tasks, they learned when the timing (to expand) was right, and they excelled at managing overall operations.

Wilson Coins Operated Machines always played according to the rules. Buffett was in charge of tax returns and other paperwork. He complied with the regulations for the business to operate legally.

Although it was 50 years ago, Warren Buffett would be happy to look back at his beginnings as a businessman. Success today comes easy to him. But, perhaps, it might have been quite different if he had failed in his first venture.

Buffett, even today, has very fond memories of his first business venture with Danly. He hasn't forgotten about the tax returns, too. In fact, reports say that he still has all of the tax returns for Wilson Coins Operated Machines.

✎ The Bond with "Cousin" Jimmy ✎

Although they share surnames, Warren Buffett and Jimmy Buffett are not related. They refer to each other as cousins during public appearances, but the monikers are all in good fun.

And, in spite of not being relatives, they formed a lasting bond.

Years' worth of friendship and admiration is founded on their love for music. Jimmy Buffett is not a stranger to the music industry.

Warren Buffett, with a musical side, would be endeared whenever his "Cousin Jimmy" performs.

Whenever the 2 of them show up on stage together, they grace the public with their instruments. Warren Buffett takes out his ukulele and Jimmy Buffett follows with his guitar.

Moreover, the friendship isn't one-sided. It's not all about music, which is Jimmy Buffett's forte. It's a give and take friendship since Warren Buffett is Jimmy Buffett's business adviser.

One time, when Jimmy Buffett considered investing in a baseball (Major League) franchise, Warren Buffett warned him of it being a bad decision. Warren Buffett's words were:

"If you're a rich guy and you buy a major league team, I mean, a really rich guy, and then you trade away one of your better players or something, or you don't pick up one that you could buy, people will say you're too cheap to get us a pennant. The whole town will get sore at you."

A Lifelong Friendship with Katharine Meyer Graham

For more than 20 years, a fierce, compassionate, and goal-oriented American publisher supervised the operations of Washington Post. She became close friends with Warren Buffett. This publisher is Katharine Meyer Graham.

The friendship started around the '70s. When Washington Post stocks became available to the public, Warren Buffett recognized the value, and approached her.

Upon the realization that both of them shared and respected each other's values, they hit it off. From the purchase of the Washington Post stocks to Katharine Meyer Graham's passing in 2001, the two have always been close friends.

In fact, their friendship attracted gossip. After all, they spent years as each other's close confidantes. For one, Buffett vacationed often in Graham's mansion in Martha's Vineyard.

Sometime, others assumed that Graham and Buffett were involved in a romantic and sexual affair. A rumor also details that Buffett's wife gave consent to a possible affair.

But, from the way both of them would talk about each other, it appears that they hadn't wanted to be anything more than friends in each other's lives. They shared a lasting friendship, and both of them appreciated that. Warren Buffett once said:

"The paper, really the company, always has been the most important thing to her."

ᴄ The Influence of Lorimer Davidsonᴄ

"An extraordinary man", says Lorimer Davidson about Warren Buffett. These words were said 15 minutes after their 1st unplanned meeting.

As mentioned in an earlier chapter, Warren Buffett met a man with whom he shared deep talks with about the insurance business. It was during the time of Benjamin Graham's rejection of his offer to work free. That was the 1st time he met a lasting influential figure, Lorimer Davidson.

Back then, Lorimer Davidson was Government Employees Insurance Company's vice-president. Warren Buffett's depth of knowledge about the insurance business impressed him. He couldn't help but pat the young Buffett's back.

That pat on the back? It was a great confidence-booster – and an unforgettable one!

"Davy", as Buffett would call him, is a very smart man. Not only did he make the young Warren Buffett confident during their 1st meeting, he exhibited effort that he wanted to be a constant friend of Buffett's.

The friendship blossomed, of course. It had to. Lorimer Davidson was a praise-worthy businessman, and Warren Buffett looked up to him.

The day of the impromptu meeting? Neither of the two men recognized the impact of bumping into each other.

If they hadn't met that day, Warren Buffett wouldn't have established a connection with the insurance company. If they hadn't met that day, there's a possibility that Warren Buffett's name would be nowhere near the names of the company's stockholders.

Years later when he could afford to take over Government Employees Insurance Company, Buffett didn't refuse. He trusted

Davidson enough to know that a deal wouldn't be put on the table unless it was a good one.

✎A Man Named William Ruane✎

Back in the days when he worked under Benjamin Graham, Warren Buffett attended a seminar that discussed the principles of value investing. At that seminar, he met William Ruane.

Buffett and Ruane became great friends. As both of them lived by Benjamin Graham's teachings, their friendship grew. Their mindsets were on to formulating better strategies as investors.

Alongside, both of them shared the philosophy of being kind to others. Since their hearts are invested in different charitable causes, they are famous figures in the industry of philanthro-capitalism or venture philanthropy.

About this welcoming nature to other people, Warren Buffett believes that those who have more and can earn more should share.

When William Ruane started his own firm, Buffett did him a big favor. Under Buffett's advice, many associates invested money in Ruane's firm.

⚬Meeting Charlie⚬

When he was about to operate his 6th partnership, Warren Buffett shook hands with Charlie Munger.

Since both of them weren't short of wit and wisdom, building rapport was a walk in the park. Buffett and Munger were like-minded individuals. They shared and respected each other's ideals. In addition, both of them resided in Omaha, Nebraska.

Shortly after they first crossed paths, Buffett and Munger became very close friends. Over the years, the two influenced each other's actions. Particularly, one reserves the right to speak his mind concerning the other's decision.

Together, they can discuss the most trivial concepts, as well as the more complex ones. They air ideas, thoughts, and opinions freely – with each of them expecting a challenge from the other.

They understand a fundamental aspect in investing: there's no single formula for a successful investment. As a duo, they're not clueless with regard to a successful prospect. They know that it's about having a partner on whom you can rely on 100%.

Fortunately, they found the reliable business partner in each other. Together, they work, and they work seamlessly.

The best part? Charlie Munger became his lifelong business partner. Munger became pivotal to Buffett's success (and vice versa).

Together, they engaged in billion-dollar deals. As Charlie Munger described their partnership, these words were said:

"If people were not often wrong, we would not be so rich."

Chapter 4- Standing Tall: The Story of Becoming a Billionaire

"No matter how great the talent or efforts, some things just take time. You can't produce a baby in one month by getting nine women pregnant."

-Warren Buffett

Once, Valley Falls Company, a textile manufacturing company operated quietly. It was a small company, but it hinted potential. Under the leadership of Oliver Chace, it generated a fairly stable profit.

Due to its potential as a growing business venture, numerous investors showed interest in the ownership of the company's stocks. With a line-up of interested parties, it started to maximize its operations. From a single headquarters back in Omaha to having offices in multiple locations, it expanded. It underwent a series of mergers, too.

Eventually it became a multinational company that provides different products and services. The list includes aerospace services, insurance, food, consumer goods, sporting gears and equipment, automotive services, and diversified investments.

Today, Valley Falls Company is one the largest companies in the United States. Today, it also goes by another name: Berkshire Hathaway, and its current CEO is Warren Buffett.

Making Millions

Due to the many partnerships he has operated, Warren Buffett's path to making millions of dollars isn't a mystery. It was in the early '60s when his partnerships had an excess of $1,025,000.

Since he believed it'd generate bigger returns, he initiated a merger. Merging his partnerships proved to be the right decision.

A controversial purchase that Warren Buffett made is one that involves an American communications company, ABC. His purchase of it was among the newsworthy subjects in the '80s. The controversy was due to the forceful nature of selling stations according to ownership rules set by the US Federal Communications Commission.

In the aforementioned deal, he played an instrumental role. Years later when another large communications company, Capital Cities, purchased ABC, he was a leading assistant with regard to the deal's success. His participation earned him a 25% commission.

The purchase of an ABC stock and the involvement in its future dealings allowed him to profit significantly. But, these couldn't be compared to the magnanimous profit he made when he purchased stocks from a popular company: Coca Cola.

With stocks from Coca Cola, Warren Buffett's high returns became predictable. After all, Coke provides beverages to billions worldwide. Currently, he owns up to 7% of the company.

✒A New Leader✒

Warren Buffett began to purchase stocks from Berkshire Hathaway in 1962. For him, it was a smart move since he used to monitor the company's standings in the stock market. Particularly, he noticed that every time the company closed one of its mills, there was a significant pattern in its price direction.

With his watchful eye over Berkshire Hathaway's standings in the stock market, he predicted its fate. He predicted that the company was in bad shape, and there was barely hope for the internal improvement of its financial situation.

At that point, he couldn't care less about Berkshire Hathaway. He refused to invest in it any more. He only retained the same shares he already owned.

When the company's current CEO (that time), Seabury Stanton, approached him, Buffett considered it an honor. Berkshire Hathaway intended to buy back the stocks from him at $11 ½ each.

The practical move was to take the offer, which was Warren Buffett's original idea. But, when he was about to sell the stocks, the price (per share) was reduced to $11 3/8.

For many people, the price change is slight, and it wouldn't make a big difference. For Warren Buffett, on the other hand, the price change showed unprofessionalism. For him, it was quite offensive.

With an angry spirit, he abandoned his original idea. It was a wise business decision to sell the stocks of the company that was about to go downhill. But, he was angry at the untoward behavior exhibited by the CEO.

Instead of selling stocks from Berkshire Hathaway, he chose to buy more (in fact, a majority) so he could be in control of the company. His plan was to have the legal power to fire the unprofessional CEO, which was eventually successful.

Apparently, Buffett realized that it was a bad call. He became emotional. Instead of just letting it slide, his anger towards the CEO drove him to make an impulsive decision. From a clear light, he could recognize the huge mistake he had just committed. He had just invested in a company that was headed to the ground. From almost every angle, it was obvious that his move was worth the negative criticism it received.

After he acquired the ownership of Berkshire Hathaway, he joined in on the company's struggle. Since he's the kind that prefers to look forward, he didn't waste time berating himself over the terrible decision he had made. Instead, he persevered to move forward with it.

Buffett strategized Berkshire Hathaway's operations. He implemented new regulations for a better managed and more profitable company. He eventually succeeded.

Since they trusted him, his partners started purchasing stocks. The company was still attractive. It also held value due to its working capital.

For a while, Berkshire Hathaway improved. With better and more effective practices, it generated a fair amount. But, after 20 years, Buffett admitted that it was doomed – if it remains as nothing but a textile manufacturing company.

Eventually, he made the decision to expand its operations. He wanted it to be in charge of offering additional products and services. From being merely a textile mill, it came a long way. The decision to delve into the industries of insurance, retail, home furnishings, railroad, newspapers, courier services, and many more proved to be a lucrative move.

Currently, it is a successful holding company that owns major businesses in America. It has an annual growth of about 20% as it serves billions of clients worldwide.

With Buffett's leadership, Berkshire Hathaway seems to be heading in a promising direction. As of 2016, its stocks are valued at more than $200,000 per share.

✄Life as a Billionaire✄

As a child, Warren Buffett's goal was to be a millionaire, which he achieved. He's the type with high hopes, but he hadn't dreamed of becoming a billionaire.

In May of 1990, he received the news that he was a paper billionaire. This means that due to the assets he owns, his net worth had reached new heights.

His billionaire status became possible when Berkshire Hathaway got into the business of marketing Class A shares. Due to the value of Class A shares, the conglomerate company attracted more investors.

A notable acquisition of Class A shares involved a global property re-insurance company, General Re-Insurance Corporation. It allowed him to generate profit, and it made him attract new audiences.

As recorded, several dealing difficulties were part of the aforementioned arrangement. If it weren't for Warren Buffett, many insurance policy holders of General Re-Insurance Corporation might not have maximized the products. Apart from helping the business succeed, he also led the way for clients to understand the products that were offered to them. Overall, he was a key figure in the resolution of issues – especially those that weren't written clearly.

As he inspected the operation of the re-insurance company, the discovery of an accounting fraud was inevitable. The accounting fraud highlighted the involvement of General Re-Insurance Company, as well as another insurance company, American International Group.

Upon close evaluation of the discovered accounting fraud, the executives from the insurance companies were implicated. The top officials of the insurance companies were flagged for improper accounting and questionable transactions. Consequently, billions of dollars went down the drain.

Although the consequence of his close inspection of the operations of General Re-Insurance Company and American International Group led to a loss, Buffett isn't worried about any conflicts that can emerge. He believes that his actions were considerably fair. He believes that the arrangement was accomplished for the sake of honest and credible service.

⚡Retaining the Billion-Dollar Status⚡

Warren Buffett is fortunate to have life work out in his favor. He's thankful that life rewards him with billions.

He's lucky, that's for sure. But, he doesn't leave matters up to luck alone. He knows that the money he owns can be gone eventually – that is, if he doesn't make an effort to keep it coming.

Here's how he manages his fortune:

- Warren Buffett still lives in the stucco home he bought back in 1958. He doesn't purchase a line-up of fancy cars, doesn't go on expensive leisure trips, and he doesn't even carry a cellular phone. Unlike other rich personalities, he refuses to build multiple mansions worldwide.

To live below his means is a trait he picked up early on. He's a cheapskate, and he prefers to be nothing else. Even if he can afford an extravagant lifestyle, he chooses to live simply.

- Buffett makes investments always – even small ones. He's quick to recognize profitable opportunities, and although he thinks big, he doesn't belittle small income opportunities.

- Buffett keeps his debts to a minimum. He knows that debts are a form of anti-investment. As a businessman, he understands that debts have negative returns, and they can't resolve most financial problems permanently.

Debt can probably help ease a crisis for a brief period. But, incurred debt can result in bad financial state. If he's eyeing a major investment, he thinks twice prior to borrowing money.

Chapter 5- Sticking by Personal Principles as an Investor

"You only have to do a very few things right in your life so long as you don't do too many things wrong."

-Warren Buffett

$\mathcal{D}$ue to his strong will and remarkable take on different issues, Warren Buffett encounters foes as an investor occasionally. And, he encounters them gladly. He's always ready to meet opposing minds. He treats them with respect, and he doesn't belittle their authority.

More importantly, he adheres to his personal principles as an investor. He tries to always remain grounded. From past experiences, he has learned to live and inspire others with the integrity he has shown in his professional life.

ꜰFamiliarization with Personal Styleꜰ

As an investor, Warren Buffett is fully aware of the industry. Particularly, he's fully aware of his personal style as an investor. He's a mix between an active and a passive investor.

From Benjamin Graham, he learned this principle – and it has proven to be classic advice. The educator taught him that to maximize his potential as an investor, he had to begin familiarizing himself with the fundamentals. He had to determine his preferred investing approach, and he had to determine how to make it work for him.

After an evaluation of his investing style, he discovered that he was an active investor. After all, he is a value investor. He has the upper hand - especially in efficient markets.

As an investor, he makes things happen when the timing is right. He's the kind who refuses to let a profitable opportunity go to waste. If he sees a logical means to profit, he'll make a move.

On the other hand, he discovered that the characteristics of a passive investor are also pre-dominant on him. He believes in the grand rewards of patience. Rather than make unprofitable moves, he can be on standby. He prefers to wait for the perfect opportunity, instead of settling for a mediocre return.

Since he's familiar with his personal style as an investor, Warren Buffett is most likely to make strategic actions. Part of his success? That could be tied to his tendency to base his moves on well-evaluated concepts. Instead of investing in products out of impulse, he ensures that matters are weighed carefully.

On Transparency

On the 2nd quarter of 2012, Warren Buffett received unsettling news. His routine test reveals that he had stage 1 prostate cancer.

After his doctors informed him that he was in bad shape, he had to implement changes. News of the nature meant that he had to approach matters slowly. He had to lighten his load, which he wasn't too thrilled about.

Aside from affecting his personal life, the news was bound to have an impact on his professional life. His ill state would attract a mix of responses from the public. He was uncertain of his peers' reaction, but he was certain of its negative impact on Berkshire Hathaway's value on the stock market.

If he chose not to relay the news of his illness to Berkshire Hathaway's shareholders, there might not be bad news with regard to the company's value. For the company to remain attractive on the stock market, he could've kept his sickness a secret. But, he refused to do that.

Warren Buffett was brave enough to divulge important information to the shareholders of Berkshire Hathaway. He chose to be transparent, and his transparency was admirable. He lived by his honest ways regardless of the consequences.

Luckily, he recovered in September of the same year. He was cancer-free. With the help of his doctors, the restoration to normal health was possible. After months of daily radiation treatment, he was as healthy as ever.

When he spoke to the public again for the first time after his treatment, he exclaimed that his energy level was back to 100%. To the shareholders of Berkshire Hathaway, as well as to the public, he was back on track.

⚞Long-Term Plans⚟

Warren Buffett invests in long-term projects since he thinks investments should be worth keeping. He appreciates all sorts of profitable opportunities, but he is more likely to go for long-term arrangements.

Notice how he rarely makes short-term engagements? For him, short-term projects are wasteful. He can profit little from them, which is a bit disrespectful to his current billionaire status. If he doesn't believe in its growing potential, he's likely to dismiss a project.

His preference for long-term projects also addresses his tendency of not purchasing luxury items. He's never the materialistic man, and he doesn't easily get beguiled by fancy belongings. If it's not a necessity, an item doesn't deserve to be spent on.

According to him, if he's interested in buying a stock, he thinks through the decision carefully. He reminds himself that if he wants to put hard-earned money on it, he should be interested in it for the long haul.

Once, he was quoted with this:

"If you aren't willing to own a stock for 10 years, don't even think about owning it for 10 minutes. Put together a portfolio of companies whose aggregate earnings march upward over the years, and so also will the portfolio's market value."

⌒Always Thinking Clearly⌒

Among the reasons for Warren Buffett's success is his clear-headedness. He always thinks from a winning perspective, but he doesn't lead himself to be blinded by idealism.

He wants to succeed in all his endeavors, and he's smart enough to realize that he has to take charge of situations. He always opts for the most sensible approach – may it be standing by an original plan or turning the other way.

Once, he said:

"Should you find yourself in a chronically leaking boat, energy devoted to changing vessels is likely to be more productive than energy devoted to patching leaks."

As an investor, he recognizes the importance of clear thinking. After acquiring the lesson from Benjamin Graham once, he applies it whenever he can. So far, the advice has proven to be timeless.

As he ventures into the stock market, he ensures that he remains realistic. For one, he's realistic with regard to market volatility. Since he knows that it's part of the business, he strategizes for volatility to work in his favor. He doesn't go against it. He knows that going against it is not worth the stress. He has learned to profit from market volatility.

With his clear mind, he's privileged to avoid a common blunder that some investors commit. When the stock market is falling, some investors panic, and they end up abandoning their original plan. As for him? Since it's not a bad thing, at all, he remains calm.

He even rejoices at the news of a depressed stock market. This means that he's able to accumulate stocks for cheap prices. Especially since he's also engaged in the food and restaurant industries, a falling stock market can be profitable for him.

In fact, together with the other investors of Berkshire Hathaway, he is happy when the market plummets. Usually, this is due to the declining prices of food. With low food prices, the company can maximize the purchase of food items, and sell them later on for higher prices.

✄ *Thinking as a Part-Owner* ✄

Every time he buys shares of a company, Warren Buffett takes the action seriously. He thinks from a high perspective. Particularly, he sees himself as part-owner of that company, rather than just a shareholder.

Remember, he's a long-term investor. This means that he's set on investing in a company's future, too. He's not the type of investor who couldn't care less about a company's condition. He doesn't merely picture himself generating money from a company.

With this kind of mentality, he's able to appreciate his investments (of a company's shares) even more. Since he believes he's part-owner, he values the company. He also refuses to sell stocks easily once he already made the purchase.

In the event that a company's fate in the stock market is about to take the plunge, he will carefully evaluate his position. If he can handle the stress due to low returns for a brief period, he'll stick it out.

For him, he's part-owner, and a part-owner doesn't quickly give up on his company. But, if it's doomed to go down after a fairly long waiting period, he'll take the initiative to make it available for selling.

⚘ Understanding Personal Level of Competence ⚘

Warren Buffett believes that his ability to understand his strengths and weaknesses grants him a competitive advantage. Over the years, he learned to capitalize on his strong points, and better himself when it comes to his weaker areas. Since he regularly assesses his own skills, he can stay within his own circle of competence.

Back in 2007 and 2008, he received criticism for allocating capital too early. His eventual strategies could've been influenced. He could've acted differently due to the public's dissatisfaction, but he didn't. Instead, he showed a collected attitude.

He believed the measures he took were just right. He doesn't doubt his actions regardless of negative bouts from others – particularly, from financial sectors.

Although Berkshire Hathaway experienced a significant downturn due to negative criticisms, Warren Buffett stuck it out at that time. Suboptimal deals became part of the transactions, but he was motivated to lead the company back up. He succeeded, of course.

Importantly, within his personal level of competence, he can generate more value. He admits that there are matters he's not good at. Instead of pressuring himself to outrank others in their niche, he focuses on his own undertakings. He's aware that another's excellent performance doesn't negate his ability to excel in a different field.

On this subject, he has been quoted to say these words:

"What an investor needs is the ability to correctly evaluate selected businesses. Note that word "selected": You don't have to be an expert on every company, or even many. You only have to be able to evaluate companies within your circle of competence. The size of that circle is not very important; knowing its boundaries, however, is vital."

Additionally, he's the type who refuses to participate in dealings that don't fall under his areas of expertise. If his skills are not useful, he won't waste his time with an investment.

✄ Decisions Are Important ✄

The ability to make wise decisions is a big part of Warren Buffett's success as an investor. He always weighs matters through, instead of participating in any profitable opportunity impulsively.

One time, he said in an interview that he prefers to spend his free time thinking and re-thinking his actions. *"An investor should act as though he had a lifetime decision card with just twenty punches on it,"* he said.

Due to the allocated time for evaluating his actions, he's trained to see the greener side of an opportunity. With regard to his professional career, he reminds himself to always act rationally.

He also acknowledges the importance of fast decision-making. In many aspects, the ability to act swiftly is an advantage. This way, he doesn't let time pass by without accomplishing a goal.

But, as Buffett believes, fast decisions might only work if they're combined with logical thinking. The idea of making fast decisions should be based on rational concepts, too.

Otherwise, decisions are quite futile. Fast decision-making without wise judgment might be rewarding, but it could only be due to luck. Reckless behavior somehow defeats the purpose of making good decisions. Sooner, he'll just regret making such bold moves, which would aggravate him.

In trading, for one, he's an arbitrage trader. Being such means he tends to maximize a profitable position immediately. He acts quickly – and wisely. If not, he will lose the temporary opportunity to profit (in small amounts) significantly.

✄ Trusting Gut Instincts ✄

Trusting his gut instincts is one of Warren Buffett's investment style. As his peers can attest, his reliance on his instincts is commendable, and it's difficult to imitate.

If he feels negatively about it, an investment's bound for dismissal. Financial advisers, stock market experts, and updated news? He doesn't base decisions on these sources. He listens, but the final word is reserved for his gut instincts.

Although he might seem so, he's not the least bit stubborn. Rather, he's strong-willed, and he's set to believe firmly in his personal strategies. If he's eyeing a prospect, he'll do the hard work himself. He'll take care of the research and evaluate a prospect's condition based on his analysis.

If need be, Buffett will go against conventional investment advice. Even if it is sensible to the others, he knows better than to hold on to an issue. Once his gut instincts warn him to discontinue an engagement, he's willing to oblige.

He prefers to keep the world and any possible distraction at bay since these can be influential. Although these factors can introduce good news, he feels more confident in his personal investment skills. After decades of being an investor, this preference of leaning on his gut has proven to be sage advice.

He admits that when he was starting out, learning to trust his gut instincts was a challenging feat. For the most part, it was a challenge since he lacked experienced as an investor. Back then, trusting himself implies that he knows better than the experienced investors.

But, even if it was challenging, he struggled to do it. He learned how to be a wise investor all on his own. Importantly, he never doubted his abilities.

"You need to divorce your mind from the crowd. The herd mentality causes all these IQ's to become paralyzed. I don't think investors are now acting more intelligently, despite the intelligence. Smart doesn't always equal rational. To be a successful investor you

must divorce yourself from the fears and greed of the people around you, although it is almost impossible," he advises aspiring investors.

✎ An Exit Strategy on Standby ✎

Warren Buffett is a man with a plan. When situations dictate that the most practical means is to let an investment go, he'll concede. He can admit defeat, but he doesn't approach matters with a defeatist attitude. He plans ahead, and an exit strategy is always part of his plan.

He always secures his positions. He is always well-prepared for the different possibilities. Instead of merely hoping for the best, he devises brilliant strategies to go out.

In the world of investing, Buffett invests with a margin of safety. He's aware that matters can possibly go haywire. If they do, he's on the safe side.

Investing with a margin of safety means that an investment is acquired for a relatively lower amount – less than the market value. So far, he has been investing this way successfully. When an investment scores unexpectedly (i.e. generates low returns), his loss is insignificant.

As a value investor, it's no surprise that he acknowledges a margin of safety whenever he invests. Having this particular exit strategy grants him the opportunity to exercise good judgment.

Chapter 6- Keeping the Success Alive

"It takes 20 years to build a reputation and five minutes to ruin it. If you think about that, you'll do things differently."

-Warren Buffet

At a young age, Warren Buffett was already a dreamer. The day when he would bathe in riches? He had always crossed his fingers for it to come.

Today, he is a wealthy man. For him, wealth is not about the money, but rather, it's more about the options that money opens up for him. With his fortune, he now has the freedom to do whatever he wants.

⚞Appreciation for Life's Bounties⚟

In his Cadillac, Warren Buffett prefers to drive himself to his appointments. As long as he's capable, he chooses not to employ someone to do work for him. He's grateful for the fact that he can still get himself to his destinations without relying on a personal driver.

This is one of the most admirable traits about him. He has an appreciative nature. Instead of chasing after more glorious victories, he persists on pragmatic ways. He appreciates and values his current possessions, and does his magic to maximize their effects.

His appreciative nature goes hand in hand with his frugal ways. As mentioned in earlier chapters, his frugality is part of his character. He's a simple man, and he's more than fine with the little luxuries that surround him.

⚞On Giving Back⚟

Another reason why Warren Buffett is cruising through life smoothly is his passion for philanthropy. He's thankful for the world's rewards, and he willingly returns the favor. According to him, he's lucky that matters worked out for him, and he wants to share that luck with the rest of humanity.

At the end of the day, his generous character allows him to be at peace. He knows that he doesn't live with greed, and he has done something to help the less fortunate ones.

Although it affected his rankings as a top contender in the world's wealthiest people, he had no second thoughts of donating billions' worth of Berkshire Hathaway shares to charity. Buffet has wowed to give away 99% of his wealth in his lifetime or within 10 years of the settlement of his estate.

Some of the recipients are:

- The Susan Thompson Buffett Foundation
- The Buffett Foundation
- The Bill & Melinda Gates Foundation
- Girls, Inc.
- Nuclear Threat Initiative
- The Sherwood Foundation
- The NoVo Foundation
- Glide
- The Howard G. Buffett Foundation

Warren Buffett (together with his friend, Bill Gates), also created a movement called the *Giving Pledge.* In this movement, he encourages billionaires worldwide to be aware of philanthro-capitalism. Particularly, he encourages them to give a hefty donation (of at least half of their fortune) to different charitable causes.

"If you're in the luckiest 1% of humanity, you owe it to the rest of humanity to think about the other 99%," he says.

◈ On Looking Fear in the Eye ◈

A major component in Warren Buffett's successful life is the ability to look fear in the eye. He knows that being fearful of something (especially if it's due to the wrong reasons) is a huge obstacle on the road towards success.

He's aware that allowing his fear to get the best of him can lead to drastic effects. Not only can fear delay his quest, it can also stop him from working forward. It occurs to him that to go near his dreams, he has to take control of his fear.

Warren Buffett learned this lesson way back when he was an educator at the University of Nebraska. Remember how he took a Dale Carnegie course on public speaking? That was the time he understood the power of self-confidence.

From that point on, he constantly reminds himself that he shouldn't let fear hold him back. For one, he's afraid of public speaking. If possible, he would miss every chance he gets to speak publicly.

But, after the lessons from the Dale Carnegie course, he strived to be a bigger person. He strived to face his fear – and he conquered it! From somebody who freaks out at the idea of public speaking, he became one of the most popular public speakers worldwide.

◈ Continually Investing in Himself ◈

Warren Buffett refuses to hit the brakes when it comes to investing in himself. Even at an old age, he continually looks out for opportunities to increase his value since he doesn't take his potential for granted.

Remember when his doctors informed him that he had cancer? Instead of merely allowing himself to be held back by his ill condition, he struggled to recover. He struggled to recover and to be in excellent shape for him to focus on his investments once more.

Once, he was quoted saying these words in an interview:

"Invest in as much of yourself as you can. You are your own biggest asset by far. Anything you do to improve your own talents and make yourself more valuable will get paid off in terms of appropriate real purchasing power. Anything you invest in yourself, you get back tenfold. Nobody can tax it away; they can't steal it from you."

As soon as he recognizes one, opportunities to learn and market himself are welcome. His attitude allows him to believe that he can always do more. He reads, he listens, and he pays attention to matters that can benefit him in the future.

⌐Always Valuing Money⌐

Warren Buffett's frugal character allows him to value money. Part of his success is tied to his practicality towards money. He stays focused and determined to retain (and add up to) his current fortune.

Like many celebrated billionaires, he acts modestly. He saves and spends only on items he permanently needs. He still forms healthy money habits for his fortune to keep increasing as time passes.

Since he considers his finesse with money-handling as an asset, he actively teaches himself tactics with regard to risk management and personal finance. He strategizes with the help of different creative ways to increase and strengthen his finances.

As he divulges in a public ceremony for the University of Florida graduates, Warren Buffett is quite lucky to have learned the habit of valuing money while he was still young. He believes that his appreciation for money is a habitual behavior that can already be very challenging to break.

For more than 6 decades, he has lived as a frugal man. For the remaining years of his life, he plans to continue his habit. As he understands, it's hardly all about luck. He believes that to maintain a particular status, he has to accomplish his part.

If he hadn't adopted such a mindset early on in life, he might not be one of the richest people in the world today. Back when he first went into business, he had $100. That $100 has definitely gone a long way.

ꕥ Moving in the Right Direction ꕥ

Buffett regularly subjects himself to self-evaluation. He knows that a regular self-check leads to wondrous and beneficial results.

Self-evaluation allows him to see himself clearly. It lets him realize his behavior, habits, and preferences. It lets him view himself, as well as the positive and negative issues about his attitude, from an unbiased perspective.

Since he assesses himself regularly, he gets to work on his flaws regularly, too. Should there be problems, he's not one to be clueless. Immediately, he turns his unpleasant habits into pleasant ones.

He admits that he committed bad calls in the past, but he knows the more important thing: he should always look ahead. After all, he learned from his old ways.

Warren Buffett is also careful about the risks he takes. He's a risk-taker, but he doesn't welcome the idea of taking uncalculated risks. He believes in the advantages of having a solid plan – and one that comes with a back-up strategy.

He knows the danger of taking big risks since he's no stranger to the negative effects of irresponsible risk-taking. He experienced having lost millions' worth of stocks. He suffered setbacks, and as he admits, the untoward actions were mainly due to greed.

"If you risk something that is important to you for something that is unimportant to you, it just doesn't make sense. I don't care if the odds you succeed are 99 to 1 or 1,000 to 1," he advised a graduating class once.

ꕥ Staying True to a Personal Definition of Success
ꕥ

For Warren Buffett, his success isn't a measurement of his fame nor his fortune. He's proud to consider himself a successful man since he achieved his childhood dream of becoming a millionaire. In fact, he has even surpassed the achievement. He out-ranked his original goal of becoming a millionaire. He attained a level above his original dream; he became a billionaire.

He doesn't compare his achievements to the achievements of others. He understands that the definition of success tends to differ from one person to the other.

He's more than satisfied with his position in life. He is in excellent health, he is in the company of great peers, he can afford to acquire his desires, and he's a highly respected man. He also has an honorable family - and he can provide well for every member. With everything going in the right turn for him, could he still ask for more?

Conclusion

ℋopefully, you have been able to get useful lessons from this book, **Warren Buffett: A Life of Inspiration**.

By pondering on the bits and pieces of his life, you can conclude that Warren Buffett is an extraordinary man. He's an extraordinary man since he chooses to be extraordinary. Not easily does he quit on different undertakings, and he's determined to always figure out a way to rise to the top.

As you've learned, Warren Buffett is a symbol of success mainly due to his winning character. For more than 6 decades as a businessman, he's not one to settle for mediocre routes. Even when he was young, he was already full of hope. He grew up aiming for big dreams.

He was a very ambitious boy but he also knew how to be grounded. The best thing about his goal-oriented trait? He ensures that he acts on them. He's not simply a wishful thinker. He perseveres, and he motivates himself to turn his dreams into reality.

Throughout his life, his persistency shows. Even after committing a few major blunders in the past, he remains standing tall – and he's doing so with confidence. He has achieved his personal goals because he was never low on determination.

Apart from learning facts about the life of Warren Buffet, hopefully you've enjoyed reading this book, too. More importantly, I hope you've been inspired to maximize your personal potential in life.

Like Warren Buffett, begin reaching success by creating a plan and strategizing. To make it big like he did, start adopting a winning attitude and learn to value your assets!

Warren Buffet's shoes are challenging to fill, but the feat's not impossible. If your heart's up for it, you'll soon come close to success,